SUZANNE DRAPER

RESILIENCE ON FOUR HOOVES

MY HORSES JOURNEY

OF RECOVERY AFTER

TRAUMATIC BRAIN INJURY

SUZANNE DRAPER

SUZANNE DRAPER

Foreword

by
Serena Ceriotti
DMV MS PhD dipl. ACVIM-LA

I share with Sue a deep passion for horses that began at a young age, despite coming from a non-horsey family. This passion has not only persisted over the years but has profoundly shaped my life, my education, and my profession as a veterinarian.

I am currently an Equine Emergency Veterinarian at Auburn University's Large Animal Teaching Hospital, where my work often carries a bittersweet nature. I have loved horses all my life, but now I tend to meet them only when they are in pain or suffering from illness.

In my role, I meet horses and their owners at some of the most difficult moments—often in the middle of the night, on weekends, or during holidays—when a critical, sometimes life-threatening, condition strikes unexpectedly. I do everything I can to help, but unfortunately, not every story has a happy ending.

Yet, the profound joy I feel with each successful recovery, and the gratitude from owners, is what motivates me to keep going, even during those long nights, holidays, and weekends when most of the world is at rest.

It was under such circumstances that I first met Sue and Marvin, on a warm late-spring Friday night in 2022. I was on call, not knowing yet that Marvin's case would become one of the most remarkable recoveries I've witnessed in my career.

Their journey became a story of resilience, dedication, and trust—a testament to the powerful bond between humans and horses, especially when navigating recovery from trauma. As a veterinarian, I find it challenging to fully express support for an owner's hope, even when I share it deeply. Objectivity and reliance on evidence-based medicine are crucial in our profession, especially when facing uncertain outcomes like those involving traumatic brain injuries. Veterinary textbooks offer little room for the emotional side of recovery, and clinical data can sometimes temper optimism. I've presented Marvin's case at conferences around the world, and my colleagues are consistently amazed by his recovery.

What made the difference, I believe, was the unshakeable bond between Sue and Marvin—their dedication, trust, and refusal to give up. That's why I'm so grateful that Sue has chosen to share their story in this book. It stands as a testament to the fact that hope is never wrong, and that commitment, day after day, step after step, truly makes a difference.

RESILIENCE ON FOUR HOOVES

I hope this book will inspire others to embrace hope, dedication, and resilience—just as it has inspired me. And tonight, as I prepare for another on call shift, it will continue to remind me why I show up every time, eager to witness many more stories like Sue and Marvin's.

Serena Ceriotti DMV MS PhD dipl. ACVIM-LA
Clinical Lecturer,
Equine Emergency Medicine and Surgery
JT Vaughan Large Animal Teaching Hospital
Auburn University
Auburn Alabama.

SUZANNE DRAPER

Acknowledgement

I would like to express my deepest gratitude to the incredible team of doctors, staff, and students at the **John Thomas Vaughan Large Animal Teaching Hospital** at **Auburn University** in Alabama. Without their expertise, care, and dedication, Marvin's recovery would not have been possible.

A special thank you to **Dr. Serena Ceriotti**, who gave me encouragement and whose skill and compassion in **Equine Medicine and Surgery** were instrumental throughout Marvin's rehabilitation. Your unwavering commitment to Marvin's well-being and your guidance through the toughest times made all the difference.

I also wish to thank **Dr. Richard J. McMullen Jr.**, the **Ophthalmologist**, for your exceptional care in addressing the challenges with Marvin's eye. Your meticulous attention to detail and determination to see him through the complications gave me hope when it was most needed.

To all the **students and staff** who supported Marvin's recovery, your dedication and kindness, along with the thorough care provided every step of the way, have left a lasting impact on Marvin's life and mine.

A heartfelt thank you to **Jennifer Martin** for stepping up during Marvin's time of need with the late-night trailer ride to

Auburn and to **Jennifer Pritchett** for making room for Marvin to have the space he needed for his recovery.

To my husband **Rob**, I owe the deepest gratitude. When everyone else thought I was mad for wanting to give Marvin a shot at recovery, you never hesitated. Your unflagging support and belief in both me and Marvin gave me the strength to push forward when it felt impossible. Also my good friends Diane Carpenter and Kelly Bergeron, my permanent support team.

This journey has been long and difficult, but with the support of such an outstanding team, Marvin is well on his way to a brighter future. For that, I am forever thankful.

Suzanne Draper & Go Marvin Go

RESILIENCE ON FOUR HOOVES

Photo Credits:
Cover: Ben Draper Photography
Story: Ben Draper Photography, Suzanne Draper

PUBLISHED BY REVOLUTION DIGITAL

No part of this publication may be copied, reproduced in any format, by any means, electronic or otherwise, without prior consent from the copyright owner and publisher of this book.

Copyright © 2024 Suzanne Draper
All rights reserved.

SUZANNE DRAPER

TABLE OF CONTENTS

Foreword 5

Acknowledgement 9

Introduction 15

Chapter 1: The Beginning 19

Chapter 2: The Incident 25

Chapter 3: The Diagnosis 33

Chapter 4: The Treatment 41

Chapter 5. Recovery and Rehabilitation 51

Chapter 6: Lessons Learned 77

Chapter 7: The Road Ahead & Conclusion 85

Chapter 8: Understanding Brain Injuries 91

Resources 99

About The Author 103

SUZANNE DRAPER

Introduction

This book was born out of one of the most challenging experiences of my life: watching my horse, Marvin, suffer a severe brain trauma. In the days and weeks following his injury, I found myself desperate for answers—searching for any information I could find on the causes of brain trauma in horses, how to care for them, what treatments might help, and what kind of rehabilitation was possible. But to my surprise, there was very little out there. I felt completely lost.

I had found Marvin as a three year old at a racehorse rescue farm in Oklahoma while searching for an off-the-track Thoroughbred (OTTB). His racing name was Go Marvin Go, though ironically, the "go" part was more like "slow." Marvin was more interested in looking at the daisies than racing other horses, so after only a few races, he was retired. After many discussions with Lynn Sullivan, the owner of Thoroughbred Athletes rescue farm, I decided to buy Marvin.

Lynn presented him as quite different to many of the other OTTB's she has been associated with over her many years in the racing industry. She described him rather than as a hot ex racehorse, as a sweet, kind, gentle horse, always inquisitive around people and wanting to be part of, or at least be close to, whatever was happening around him.

I had him delivered, sight unseen, to the barn I was associated with in Georgia. I hadn't met him in person yet, but I knew from our conversations that he had the potential for a new career in dressage and eventing.

As someone who has owned, competed and cared for horses my entire life, Marvin's brain injury was unlike anything I had ever faced before. I documented every step of our journey, from the moment of the injury to the long months of recovery that followed. Each decision, each setback, and each small victory became a part of a learning process that I had to navigate largely on my own.

What struck me most as I began sharing Marvin's story with fellow equestrians was how many people wanted to know more. Everyone who met Marvin following the injury had questions—about his care, his treatment, and what his future would hold. It became clear that there was a need for this kind of information, and I knew that our story could offer both guidance and hope to others who might one day face a similar situation.

That's why I've written this book. It's not just about Marvin's brain injury; it's about the uncertainty, the perseverance, and the patience that comes with caring for a horse through a traumatic experience.

It's about what worked for Marvin—what helped him heal and what challenges we faced along the way.

Through this book, I hope to provide insight into the care and rehabilitation of a horse after a brain injury. Whether you're an equestrian looking for information or simply someone who loves horses, my goal is to share our journey and hopefully provide the guidance that was so hard for me to find

Suzanne and Marvin before the accident

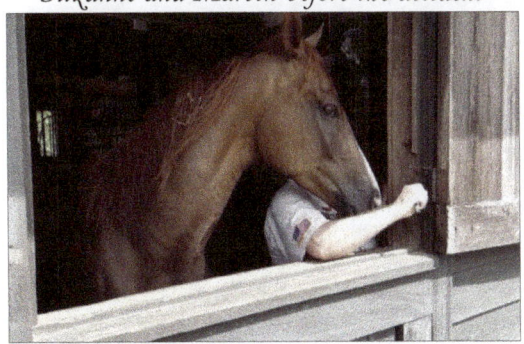

Marvin inspecting repair work.

SUZANNE DRAPER

Chapter 1: The Beginning

Horses have always held a special place in my life. From the time I was about eight years old, I have been riding. My journey with horses began in Pony Club in Australia, where I learned the fundamentals of riding and horse care. As I progressed, so did my ambitions—I moved into the world of three-day eventing and dressage, disciplines that challenged both horse and rider to be in perfect harmony. Riding was not just a hobby; it became a central part of my life, shaping who I am.

The First Encounter

After relocating from California to Georgia, I found myself searching for something familiar to ground me in my new surroundings. Moving across the country had brought excitement, but also a sense of uncertainty. That's when I discovered a racehorse rescue farm in Oklahoma and came across Marvin.

Marvin was different from the other horses at the rescue. His tall, lean frame and powerful muscles spoke of his racing heritage, but there was a calmness in his eyes that intrigued me.
He wasn't skittish or high-strung like some of the other ex-racers. Instead, he seemed to carry a quiet dignity and a calmness I knew he would be fun.

First turnout in Georgia

The Early Days

Bringing Marvin back to Georgia was the beginning of a new chapter for both of us. As a former racehorse, Marvin had been trained for speed and competition, but my vision for him was different.

My goal was to move him into dressage and, eventually, three-day eventing. However, I knew that before we could reach those heights, there would be a lot of groundwork to do.

We started slow. I had to help Marvin unlearn the habits of his racing career and adjust to a new way of moving, a new pace.
Groundwork became our foundation, with a focus on teaching him to relax, to carry himself differently, and to develop a more balanced, responsive frame.
It was a big shift from the world he had known, but Marvin proved to be a quick learner. His willingness to adapt was remarkable, and I could see the potential in him every time we worked together.

Building Trust

As with any horse, trust is something that develops over time, and with Marvin, it was no different. Our early work wasn't just about physical training—it was about building a bond of trust and understanding.

The groundwork sessions were crucial in establishing this trust. I began with free lungeing in a round pen, something I had never done before.
We worked on basic exercises like lungeing, learning to soften at the bit, and developing rhythm and balance at slower gaits.

Each session was a lesson for both of us. I had to remind myself to be patient, to understand that Marvin's instincts had been shaped by his racing past. Slowly, he began to respond—not just to my commands, but to my presence, to the unspoken communication that exists between horse and rider.

I remember one early session in particular. It was a chilly morning, and Marvin was full of energy. He was trotting on the lunge line, his head held high as if he were still at the racetrack.
But as the session progressed, I could see him start to relax. His head dropped slightly, his gait became more measured, and he began to listen. It was a small but significant moment—one that marked a turning point in our journey together.

The Bond

Over time, our bond deepened. Marvin wasn't just learning new skills; he was learning to trust me, and I was learning to trust him. His progress was slow but steady, and with each passing day, I could see the potential for him to excel in dressage and eventing. We were building a partnership that would extend beyond the arena.

My experience from years of riding and competing helped guide me, but Marvin brought his own wisdom to the table.

RESILIENCE ON FOUR HOOVES

There were moments when his racing instincts would reappear, when the need for speed would kick in and I'd have to remind him to slow down, to focus. But then there were moments of pure harmony, where everything seemed to click, and I could feel Marvin embracing this new chapter of his life just as I was.

Little did I know that our bond, and the progress we had made, would soon be tested in ways I never could have anticipated. Our journey together was about to take a turn that would challenge everything I thought I knew about horses, health, and healing.

SUZANNE DRAPER

Chapter 2: The Incident

It started out as a completely normal day, one that didn't seem like it would be any different from the hundreds of others I had spent with Marvin. I headed to the barn and spent the morning working him as usual. We focused on some basic dressage flatwork, refining our communication and practicing transitions. Marvin was his typical self—responsive, eager to work, and moving well. After we finished, I hosed him down, letting the cool water run over his muscles as he cooled off from the session. He stood quietly as I rinsed him, a calmness between us that always followed a good ride.

Once he was cooled off, I turned him out in the paddock with his two "mates" he was usually with, then headed home. It was a routine I had followed many times before, nothing out of the ordinary. As I drove home, I made a quick stop at the ATM, never imagining that everything was about to change.

The Call

I was standing at the ATM when my phone rang. It was the barn owner.

Her voice was tight with urgency, and I could immediately tell that something was wrong. "Marvin's had a fall," she said. "He won't get up. You need to come back immediately."

My heart raced as her words sunk in. Marvin wouldn't get up? It was hard to comprehend. He was fine when I left the barn—healthy, strong, moving well.
What could have possibly happened in the short time since I had turned him out? I abandoned my errand and rushed back to the barn, dread filling my thoughts.

Arriving at the Barn

When I arrived at the barn, the tension in the air was palpable. The barn owner met me and quickly filled me in. She had been out mowing the fields and had seen Marvin galloping with the two other horses in the paddock. Everything seemed fine at first—just three horses enjoying the freedom of the field. Then, in an instant, it all changed. One moment, Marvin was running, and the next, she noticed he was down. He wasn't getting back up.

I hurried over to the paddock, and there he was—on his feet now, but something was very wrong. Marvin stood shakily, his legs trembling as he struggled to balance himself. He wasn't moving, just standing in place as though unsure how to take a step. His eyes were flickering, darting around without focus, and there was no recognition in them. It was as if he didn't know where he was or what had happened.

Trying to Piece It Together

The barn owner and I tried to make sense of what had happened.
From what she had seen, Marvin and the other horses had been running, their usual playful energy carrying them across the paddock. But something must have gone wrong. Maybe Marvin had reared up, lost his footing, and fallen backward. It was the only explanation that made sense, though we couldn't be sure. He and Goose often reared playfully when together.

What worried me most was how Marvin was acting now. Everything looked fine at first glance except for his unsteady posture—there were no obvious signs of injury. His legs seemed unhurt, there were no cuts, scrapes or swelling, and his coat looked clean, as if nothing had happened.

But Marvin was completely different from the horse I had left just an hour before. He was standing, but he wasn't truly present. His body was swaying slightly, and his eyes kept flickering, unable to focus. It was as though he was struggling to stay upright, using every ounce of his energy just to balance himself.

The Urgency of the Moment

It took almost three hours for the vet to arrive, and for every single minute of that time, we stayed right beside Marvin.

We didn't dare try to move him. The fear that he might collapse and not be able to get up again was overwhelming. His legs were trembling beneath him, and though he was standing, it was clear that he was on the edge of losing his balance at any moment.

What made it even more unsettling was that Marvin made no attempt to move. He just stood there, almost frozen in place. There were no signs of him wanting to walk, to lie down, or even to graze. His complete stillness was eerie, as though he instinctively knew that any attempt to move could make things worse.

The minutes dragged on as we waited for the vet, each one feeling like an hour. I spoke to Marvin softly, trying to reassure him, but there was no response.

His eyes continued to flicker, his body swayed gently in the breeze, and every few moments I feared he would collapse. All we could do was wait.

The Unknown

When the vet finally arrived in the late afternoon, we carefully walked Marvin to the barn so the vet could perform a thorough check. Every step was a struggle for him, and I kept a firm hand on his lead, afraid he might fall at any moment. Once inside the barn, the vet got to work. After a detailed physical examination, he decided to X-ray Marvin's neck to rule out any spinal injuries. Thankfully, the X-rays didn't show any fractures or dislocations, but the vet's expression remained serious.

He gave Marvin some medication to help with the pain and possible swelling in the brain if in fact it existed. He then pointed out the one thing I had feared the most: Marvin's flickering eyes. According to the vet, this was a clear sign of brain trauma, most likely caused by a fall.

The vet advised us to place Marvin in a space larger than a typical stall. If he were to fall again, we needed to ensure there was enough room to help him get up. A small space could make things worse if he collapsed.

The vet gave him more medication to help with any potential swelling in the brain and urged me to keep a close watch on him through the night.

Marvin unsteady in the round pen.

By now, it was getting dark, but I wasn't going to leave Marvin alone. I decided to stay with him overnight. I brought a chair out to the round pen where he was resting and settled in for what would be a long night. As I sat there, watching him in the dim light, I noticed something else—Marvin's right eye was getting cloudy and quite red. It didn't look right, and it only added to my growing concerns.

The barn owner agreed that Marvin needed more attention. She suggested that I take him to John Thomas Vaughan Large Animal Teaching Hospital at Auburn University in Alabama.—about 80 miles away.

I didn't hesitate. I called the Hospital, and they said to bring him down immediately. The problem was, it was now 8 PM, and I didn't have a trailer. The owners trailer was in Florida. I made a few frantic calls, but with no luck. Finally, I reached out to my friend Jennifer, who was having dinner at a local restaurant. Without a second thought, she said she would go home, get her trailer, and be out as fast as possible.

When Jennifer arrived, we faced another problem: Marvin was having great difficulty trying to step up into the trailer. The trailer was a step-up model, and with his shaky legs, it seemed almost impossible for him to get his footing. We tried several times, but Marvin just couldn't manage the step.

Finally, we backed the trailer up to a mound of gravel, creating a makeshift ramp. With my help, placing one foot after the other into the trailer, and waiting for him to feel secure, he was able to get into the trailer, and we finally got him loaded. It was a huge relief, but I couldn't shake the fear that Marvin might not survive the trip.

The Drive to Auburn

We began the 2 hour drive to Auburn at around 10pm, hoping that the specialists there could give me the answers—and the treatment—that Marvin so desperately needed.
We arrived at the University Veterinary Center around midnight, where we were met by the vet on call. Exhausted but focused, we carefully walked Marvin into the ICU. Watching him struggle with each step tore at my heart, but finally, we got him settled into the clinic.

At that point, all I could do was wait. The vet assured me they would begin their analysis right away, but I felt completely helpless. I left for the long drive back home, hoping to catch a few hours of rest before returning for an update on Marvin's condition.

When I arrived home at around 4 AM, I was met with an empty house. My husband, Rob, was in Canada working on a movie, and for the first time since the ordeal began, the weight of it all hit me. With thoughts racing through my mind, my emotions let go. I sat alone in the quiet of our home, tears streaming down my face, feeling utterly overwhelmed.

The silence of the house only deepened my feelings of helplessness, and I was unable to sleep, no matter how hard I tried. I waited for hours, consumed with worry, praying that Marvin was in good hands and that I'd receive the call soon with an update on his condition. All I could do was wait and hope for the best.

Chapter 3: The Diagnosis

After a short and sleepless night, my phone finally rang with the update I had been anxiously waiting for. It was the first call from the Veterinary Hospital since I had left Marvin in their care. I barely registered the time as I answered, my heart pounding in my chest, desperate for any news about Marvin's condition.

The vet on the line informed me that Marvin had been placed into the Intensive Care Unit (ICU) overnight. They had immediately started him on a non-steroidal anti-inflammatory (NSAID) drip to help manage the pain and reduce any swelling in his brain. This was a precautionary measure to prevent further complications while they conducted rigorous and extensive testing to determine the extent of his injuries.

Hearing the word "ICU" sent a chill through me. While I had known Marvin's condition was serious, it was now sinking in just how critical the situation was. My mind was swirling with worst-case scenarios, but I held on to the hope that the tests would reveal something treatable—something we could fight.

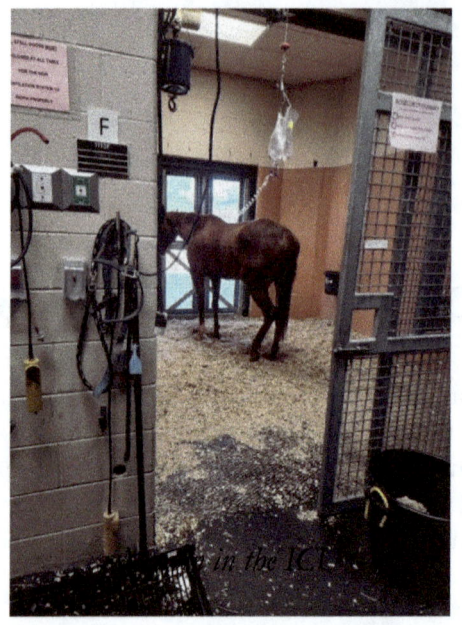

in the ICU

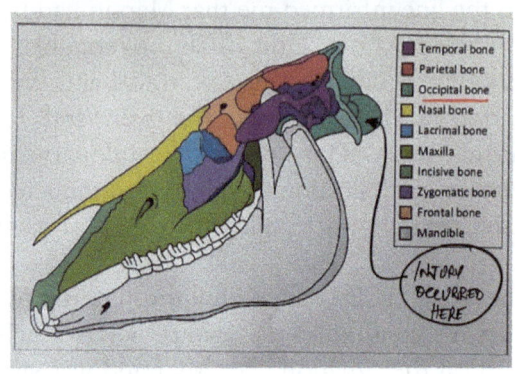

The First Round of Tests: Day 1 (5/28/2022)

After an overnight stay in the ICU, Marvin underwent a thorough examination.

The Vet's findings were as follows:

Marvin was bright, alert, and responsive. He was in good body condition with a body score of 5/9, with adequate and symmetric muscling. He was slightly tachycardic (having an abnormally fast heart rate), with a heart rate of 56 beats per minute and a respiratory rate of 38 beats per minute, but he had a normal rectal temperature of 98.6 degrees Fahrenheit. His mucous membranes were pink and moist, with a normal capillary refill time of less than 2 seconds. A distal small fracture was observed on the tooth 102. A complete neurological examination was performed. Marvin's mental status appeared normal. Complete blood cell count and blood chemistry did not reveal any abnormalities.

Dynamic examination revealed severe proprioceptive ataxia (lack of coordination due to sensory deficits) in all limbs, grade 3-4/5, characterized by circumduction (circular movement of the limb) of the hind limbs and frequent crossing of the forelimbs at the walk. Additionally, mild signs of right-sided vestibular ataxia (disorder affecting balance) were intermittently noted, including leaning and falling toward the right.

An evaluation of Marvin's right eye was performed thoroughly the morning after admission in collaboration with the equine ophthalmology service. A superficial but extensive corneal ulcer was identified with fluorescein staining.

No signs of uveitis or infections were detected, but only partial myosis (constriction of the pupil).
The left eye was normal. Based on the physical examination and diagnostic performed, Marvin was presumptively diagnosed with traumatic brain injury and traumatic right corneal ulcer.

Based on the concurrent presence of a right-sided vestibular syndrome (disorder affecting balance) and proprioceptive ataxia, a central brain origin of the neurological signs was considered likely. With probable localization of the lesion at the level of the brain stem, skull radiographs were taken on 5/31/22 and revealed the presence of a small avulsion (a fragment of bone pulled away by a tendon or ligament) fracture of Marvin's basi-occipital bone. This finding was consistent with the presumptive traumatic etiology (cause of disease or condition) and the suspected location of the neurological lesion.

Marvin was hospitalized in a special neurological padded stall in the intensive care unit for monitoring and medical management. Marvin was otherwise hourly monitored for changes in attitude, deterioration of his neurological signs, signs of colic, appetite, water consumption, urination, and defecation. A complete physical examination was performed every 12 hours throughout his hospitalization.

The Waiting Game

As the Doctor spoke, I felt my emotions teetering between hope and despair. The first wave of testing had provided some answers but not the full picture. More tests were on the way, and I knew that I would be waiting for what felt like an eternity for the next update.

I asked the Doctor how Marvin was responding to the treatment so far. She said he was stable but quiet, still showing signs of disorientation. The anti-inflammatory drip was helping to control swelling, but it would take time before they could assess whether it was having the desired effect on his overall condition.

Brain Trauma in Horses

During our conversation, the vet explained more about equine brain trauma and how complex it could be. Horses, with their large skulls and long necks, are particularly vulnerable to head and neck injuries. A fall like Marvin's—where his head might have struck a hard surface—can result in anything from mild concussions to more serious traumatic brain injuries. The symptoms Marvin was displaying, like the flickering eyes and unsteadiness, were signs of neurological damage, but determining the severity of the injury would take time.

The vet mentioned that in many cases, horses with brain trauma could recover, but the speed and extent of their recovery would depend on the level of damage and how quickly the swelling could be brought under control. Being a young horse was at least one thing in his favor for a positive recovery.

The Long Road Ahead

Before ending the call, the vet reassured me that Marvin was in good hands and that they would continue to monitor him around the clock.

They still had more tests to run, and they would adjust his treatment plan as they learned more about his condition.
For now, it was a waiting game—waiting for his body to respond to the medication and for the tests to reveal the full extent of his injury.

I thanked the vet, hung up the phone, and sat in silence. It was all so overwhelming—knowing that Marvin was fighting something so big, something invisible, and all I could do was wait. I felt helpless, caught between hope and fear, bracing myself for whatever news would come next.

The biggest unknown was if Marvin would actually recover. There were no guarantees that he would recover or, if he did recover somewhat, he may never be able to be ridden again.

Several friends suggested having him euthanized due to both the cost of treatment and the uncertainty of his recovery.

However, after talking it through with my husband, Rob, we decided to go ahead, as I was confident (probably hoping more than confident) that he would recover and I would be able to get him back into work and rebuild his fitness. I felt he deserved a chance, and I was determined he would get that chance.

Our first goal was to get through his treatment and then give him six months, after which we could reevaluate. It was an awful accident, but it did not feel like it should be life-ending, so I pushed forward.

RESILIENCE ON FOUR HOOVES

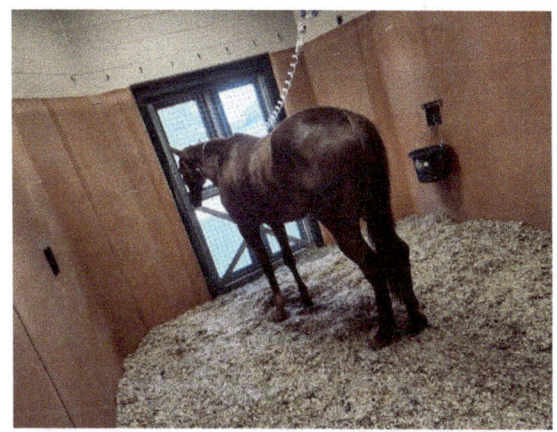

Marvin in ICU connected to IV

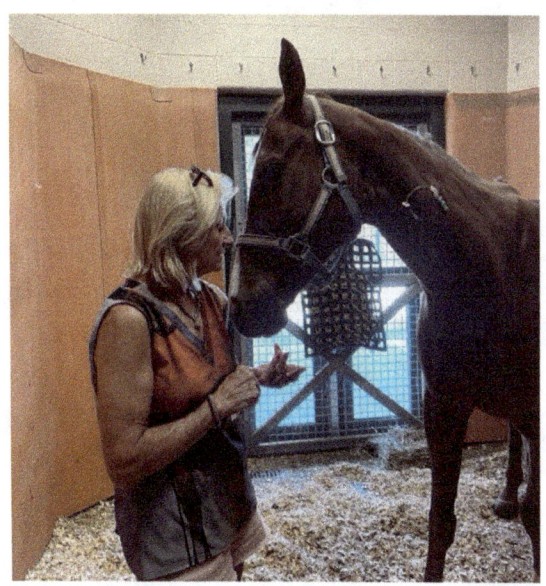

Visiting Marvin every two days in the ICU

SUZANNE DRAPER

Chapter 4: The Treatment

Once the diagnosis was clear, Marvin's treatment plan began immediately. The veterinarians knew that the road to recovery would be long and uncertain, but their focus was on reducing the swelling in his brain and giving his body the best chance to heal. The next few days were critical, and every decision had to be carefully made with Marvin's well-being in mind.

The staff at the University Veterinary Hospital said I could visit Marvin whenever I wanted, and as I initially thought he would only be there for one week to 10 days, I decided to drive the 160-mile round trip every two days. I could only spend about 20 minutes with him each day as I had to have someone from the clinic with me and I could not take up too much of their time. However, given the trauma and the foreign environment, I wanted Marvin to know I was still there for him. Little did I know the week to 10 days would turn into one month and thousands of miles driving back and forth, due to complications with Marvin's eye.

Monitoring and Neurological Management

Marvin was placed in a neurological padded stall to reduce the risk of injury if he became unsteady or fell.

He was monitored hourly for changes in his neurological condition—any deterioration could be a sign of further complications, such as increased pressure on his brainstem or a secondary injury. The veterinary staff kept track of his appetite, water consumption, urination, and defecation. It was essential that his body functioned properly during this critical time. A complete physical examination was performed every 12 hours to check for any changes in his overall condition, particularly in his neurological signs.

Hourly Monitoring Included:

Attitude: Was Marvin responsive, alert, or lethargic?
Neurological Signs: Any new signs of ataxia (unsteady movement) or disorientation.
Appetite: Did he show interest in food or water?
Bowel Movements and Urination: Were his digestive and urinary systems functioning normally?
Signs of Colic: Any signs of discomfort or pain, which could complicate his recovery.

The team was also prepared to adjust his treatment if there were any signs of deterioration, knowing that even a small change could signal a major shift in Marvin's condition.

Addressing the Corneal Ulcer

Marvin's right eye, which had been diagnosed with a traumatic corneal ulcer, required specialized treatment as well.

The ophthalmology team prescribed an antibiotic ointment to prevent infection and encourage healing. They also used an atropine solution to dilate his pupil and relieve some of the discomfort caused by the ulcer.

Marvin's eye was treated every hour initially and as time went on he became increasingly more difficult to catch. I guess he was getting tired of the constant prodding and poking he had to put up with each time his eye was treated. At least he was reacting so I saw that as a positive sign…..a small win as far as I was concerned.

Initially, it was thought Marvin might be ready to be discharged around the 8th of June, but concerns arose when the ophthalmologist suspected an infection in his eye.

They decided to perform a culture, and the results confirmed the presence of bacteria on the ulcer.

To address this, the vets inserted a **subpalpebral lavage system** (SPL) to deliver medication directly to the eye, ensuring it reached the affected area more effectively. The SPL is a small tube placed under the eyelid, allowing medication to be administered frequently without having to disturb the eye itself. The tube is long and attached to the mane so medication can be easily injected without touching the eye. Marvin was given aggressive therapy every four hours to combat the infection and promote healing.

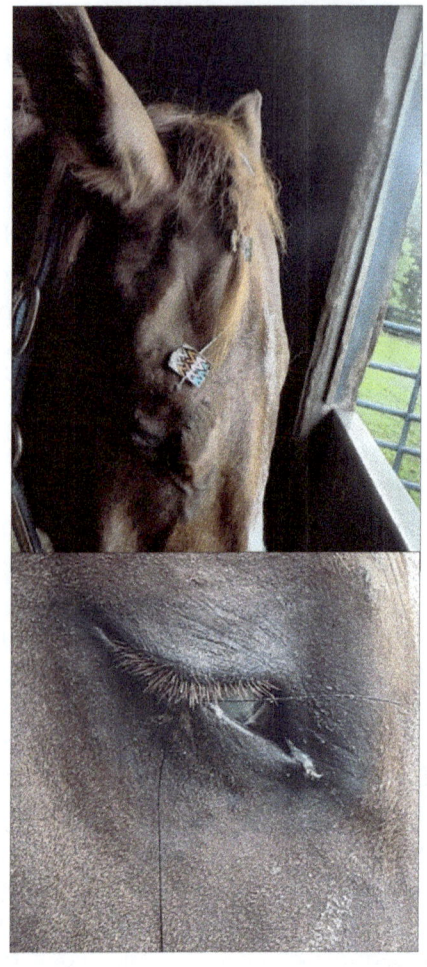

Marvin with SPL tube inserted and eye stitched

RESILIENCE ON FOUR HOOVES

From my Diary:

Things started to improve. The IV was removed on 6/18 and his medication was decreased. The ulcer and corneal edema were getting smaller. However, his tear production was significantly reduced. We were hoping he would be released soon, but only time would tell. He was moved from the ICU to another barn on 6/21, still a padded stall but more like a normal stall, to prepare him for being discharged and returning home.

Each day he was taken for a walk outside and a pick of grass. His walking wasn't too bad, not 100% straight, still a little wobbly but getting better.

It's now June 23rd, and the ophthalmologist is concerned about his corneal ulcer. It appeared to be getting worse. It looked infected and was showing more bacteria.

I met with the ophthalmologist on the 23rd to discuss Marvin's eye, and it seems he may need a graft. With surgery, it would heal in a week or so; without it, it could take a month. That night he went into surgery, but the doctor decided not to do the graft as it would have been too large and there was too much unhealthy tissue. Instead, his eye was aggressively debrided, and a contact lens was placed to protect the injured eye. His eye was temporarily stitched closed at the same time to help retain the contact lens. What else could go wrong?

Marvin remained in the hospital for another four days, and it finally looked like I would take him home with the SPL, contact lens, and stitches still in his eye. He would need to return to have them removed.

From the Hospital Notes:

On 6-27-2022, we removed the suture to take one final look at the eye and evaluate its healing before we released him. The corneal ulcer had decreased greatly in size and was about 50% smaller than it was on Friday.

The epithelial margins were smooth, meaning that the epithelium was growing back properly with no complications. New vessels were extending down to the cornea ulcer to provide extra support as this area heals. We are very happy to see such rapid progress in his healing and we believe that it carries a very good prognosis for the quick resolution of this ulcer.

Rehabilitation and Gradual Movement at the Hospital.

Once Marvin stabilized, the next focus was rehabilitation. Due to the proprioceptive ataxia (lack of coordination) caused by his brain injury, Marvin's ability to move normally was compromised. His rehabilitation had to be handled delicately to avoid further injury while encouraging his brain to relearn coordination.

The initial phase involved restricted movement. Marvin was kept in his stall for several days, with only brief, slow walks under close supervision. Each step had to be monitored to ensure that his balance was improving and that he wasn't at risk of falling.

As time passed, the walking sessions were gradually lengthened. Marvin's balance remained shaky, but the veterinarians reassured me that improvement would come with time and patience.

These early walks were critical in helping his brain regain its ability to control his limbs.

The Emotional Rollercoaster

The early days of treatment were a rollercoaster of emotions. Some days, Marvin would seem alert and responsive, giving me hope that he was turning a corner.

But other days, his ataxia would worsen. Each day the Vet's would take him outside for a pick of grass. When I visited I was permitted to lead him but always with supervision….just in case. Sometimes, when walking him, I would have to keep him at arm's length to be sure he didn't stumble and fall toward me. He was definitely more sensitive when he heard sounds that were once normal but were now apparently very scary.

Every phone call from the vet brought a wave of anxiety. There were constant updates—both good and bad—and I couldn't help but prepare myself for the possibility that Marvin might not recover fully. Brain trauma is unpredictable, and while the vets were cautiously optimistic, no one could give me a definite answer about his long-term prognosis.

Adjusting Treatment as Needed

The vet team was highly attentive, making adjustments to Marvin's treatment as his condition fluctuated. After the first week, they gradually reduced the corticosteroids, monitoring for any changes in swelling or neurological signs.
His NSAID drip was continued, but they began introducing oral medications that he could continue taking at home once discharged.

One key aspect of Marvin's treatment was managing his environment. He needed peace and quiet, with minimal stress or stimulation. The padded stall reduced the risk of injury if he fell, and the limited movement kept him safe while allowing his body time to heal. This, combined with the close monitoring, gave him the best chance for recovery.

Marvin didn't lay down for about one week, which is quite normal. Horses instinctively know when they are not able to get up so they don't put themselves in that position. Everyone at the Hospital was elated when he did lay down and easily got back up. This was a very good sign.

Looking Forward

As the days passed, the small victories started to add up. Marvin's balance slowly improved, and his appetite returned.

His right eye, though still healing, showed signs of improvement. He was far from being out of the woods, but for the first time since the injury, I began to feel a small spark of hope.

The treatment phase was far from over, but Marvin's progress, however slow, was encouraging. Each step forward gave me more confidence in his ability to recover, though I knew the road ahead would still be challenging.

It was finally time to take Marvin home, but that was going to provide new challenges and a move to another barn.

Notes from Vet Hospital Discharge Papers:

Follow up and Prognosis:

We recommend working with a local veterinarian who can easily recheck Marvin's neurological examination at regular intervals. If Marvin improves enough and the goal is to be ridden again, we recommend performing a CT scan of his head to further evaluate for fracture healing or any other possible injuries that could not be highlighted in the radiographs during this hospitalization. Marvin's prognosis for athletic use is guarded. Neurologic injuries can take many months to reach the full extent of improvement. Marvin should not be ridden or driven by anyone unless a normal neurological examination has been confirmed by a veterinarian.

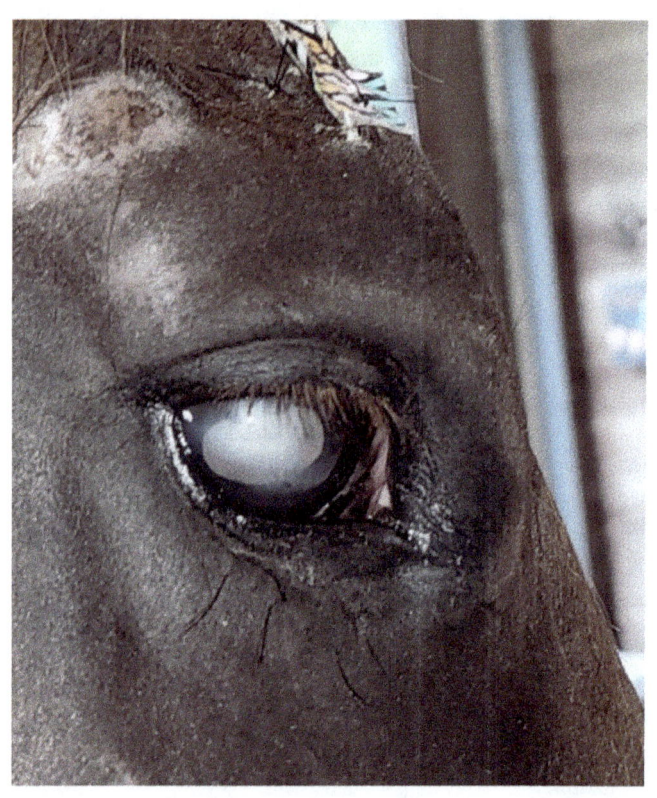

Marvin's eye with stitches removed and SPL still in place

Chapter 5. Recovery and Rehabilitation

The recovery and rehabilitation process for Marvin was one of the most challenging and unpredictable experiences of my life. When you're dealing with an injury as serious as traumatic brain injury, every day is a test of patience and perseverance. The path forward was never straight, and it required both Marvin and me to adapt to a constantly shifting reality.

The First Day After Returning Home

The biggest initial challenge was that the vet's wanted Marvin confined to a stall and small yard so his movement would be limited. The barn where the injury occurred did not have that kind of setup, so I needed to find another barn that could accommodate him. This was a difficult and stressful transition, now taking him to a new home with no familiarities, as I had to ensure that Marvin's new environment met the specific needs outlined by Dr Ceriotti.

Note from Hospital: *"Please keep Marvin confined to a stall and small paddock. This area should be small enough that he cannot canter or gallop around with too much speed. The area should have good firm flat footing to make it easier for Marvin to navigate the environment and reach his water and feed areas."*

After securing a new location, I was able to bring Marvin home, but the journey was far from over. I found a barn, funnily enough owned by yet another Jennifer, not too far from my home.

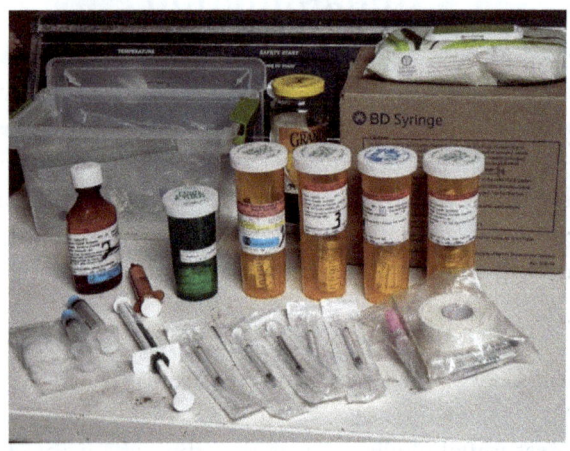

I had to thoroughly strip the stall of anything Marvin could possibly get caught on, and we made a small makeshift yard from round pen panels so he had a small yard during the day and could be locked in at night.
The goal was to have the flexibility to make the yard larger as Marvin hopefully progressed.

Building a Rehabilitation Plan

Marvin's neurological symptoms remained a central concern throughout his rehabilitation. His coordination was still unsteady, but getting better, and I had to be especially careful when leading him in and out of the stall or when turning him out into the paddock.

One of the most noticeable signs of his injury was his tendency to lean or drift toward the right. This was a lingering effect of the brain trauma, likely due to the vestibular system being affected. I also had to be more careful approaching Marvin on his right side.

My goal was to get Marvin back to normal despite the doom and gloom presented by everyone else, but I still realized he may never recover. However, I had faith in my ability and in Marvin's resilience. Once he was settled in, I started on a daily routine of letting Marvin out so he could walk in his yard, and every day I made sure to take him for a walk. I wanted to ensure he was always doing more than he would if left on his own. I was determined not to just leave him or turn him out for six months, just to see what would happen.

I felt that would not result in any progression, or a much slower progression than if he was pushed to do some work. I was determined to make his recovery a reality.

At first, I really wasn't sure how to approach this. There were no books and very few articles about recovery from equine brain injury, so I had to devise my own plan, inventing exercises with increasing degrees of difficulty, still very basic, I figured would help him recover.

I knew Marvin had to be moving and working his muscles, so we started walking short distances in straight lines. He was still a little off balance, so I walked him up and down a driveway on fairly flat ground, increasing the amount of time each day by about five minutes until we were doing 20-minute walks on a daily basis.

I had to be very cautious of him falling towards me, particularly when he saw something unusual or heard a sound. For the first couple of weeks, everything in the world was new to him again, and it was exacerbated by the fact he was in a new environment. As he became more settled on the walks we started upping it to two walks each day

Stepping it Up and More Groundwork

As Marvin started to become more steady and sure on his feet, I began taking him on walks where the ground was more uneven, which forced him to use more muscles and engage his brain. I also introduced large circles and walked up and down the banks on the side of the dam.

Eventually, we even started taking him on walks with another horse, with Jennifer riding her horse and me walking with Marvin. He was definitely showing incremental signs of improvement, but he still had a significant tilt in his head and neck to the right, which was especially noticeable when he was in his stall.

One of Marvin's first walks on uneven ground.

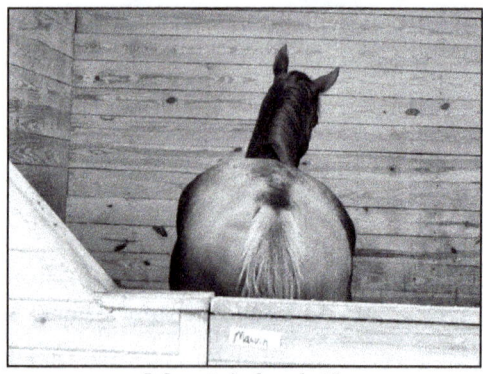

Marvin's head tilt.

Through July and August, I made the yard progressively larger by adding more round pen panels and finally let Marvin into the larger paddock, removing all the panels. He had now gone from what was essentially a 15'x15' yard to a 30'x40' yard where he was able to move more freely and seemed to be having no problem cantering around and making reasonably tight turns. His head was still tilting to the right, and he would overreact to unusual or loud sounds.

Progressively larger yards made from round pen panels.

RESILIENCE ON FOUR HOOVES

I had a chiropractor start working with Marvin now as he was much more stable and I felt she could give me insights into his progress and point to areas on which I needed to work, more specifically, to assist in Marvin's recovery. At this point he was becoming much easier to handle and be around and I was not worried about lack of balance. He was definitely improving.

All this time I continued to treat his right eye, which still had the SPL tube attached. The eye remained quite cloudy but was slowly improving, and he was not nearly so reactive when approached from the right side, indicating he was seeing much better.

On July 5th, I took Marvin to Auburn Hospital to have his eye re-checked by the Ophthalmologist.

Note from Hospital: *"We took the sutures out that were holding the eyelids closed and removed the contact lens. On examination, we noted a large bed of granulation tissue and some blood vessels within the cornea. This gives us the indication that Marvin's cornea is healthy as it is undergoing proper healing. When we applied fluorescence stain to the right eye, no deficits in the cornea were noted. At this time, we believe that the ulcer is completely healed."*

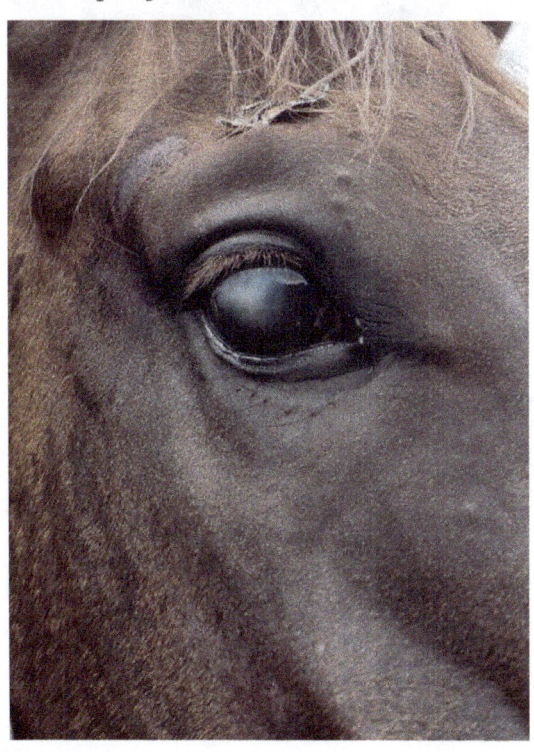

On August 10th, the SPL was removed, and I had to continue adding drops to his eye to help with tear production. He adapted well to the routine and it was no problem at all when placing the drops in his eye.

In August, I decided to move him to a barn with other horses, next to his paddock where he was locked in at night and turned out in the 30'x40' yard during the day. I also started turning him out _beside_ other horses, and he would play over the fence, seeming quite stable. However, the Doctors stressed that I should definitely not put him out _with_ another horse.

Marvin was happy to have his playmate back

Following another Ophthalmology checkup to the hospital on August 31st, Marvin's eye looked great. It showed a moderate amount of scarring, but the ophthalmologist was very pleased with the healing and tear production.
He felt his eye would improve over time but might have a permanent scar for the rest of his life. He needed to remain on the I-Drop Vet Plus once per day in both eyes.

May 2023 Almost one year later Marvin's right eye looking great (picture over page).

Eye Looking Better

Over the next few months, I started working Marvin in the round pen.
First of all, with no gear and just having him walk, trot, and canter both directions, and he seemed to be doing fine. Gradually, I added a lungeing surcingle and a bridle, and just free-worked him in the round pen.

As Marvin became more comfortable with the surcingle and the bridle, I started using the lunge line, and he responded well. He didn't seem to be having any issues being able to walk, trot, and canter both directions very easily.

At that point, I decided to start putting gear on him as if I was riding, so I removed the surcingle, put a saddle, bridle, side reins, and was able to lunge him no problem at all. To give Marvin the sensation of extra weight, without me getting on, I added a 10lb leather lead weight bag I used back in the day for eventing, to bring my weight up to the minimum weight required for competition.

Finally, I started lungeing in the big arena, and bit by bit he was improving all the time. However I could still notice a head tilt, and he was still quite reactive to sounds.

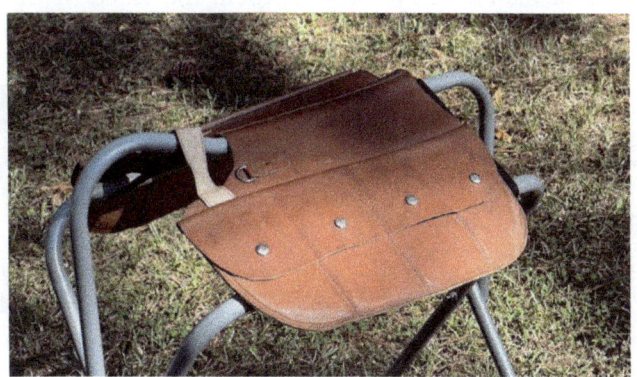

Weight Bag

By mid-December, I decided Marvin was going pretty well. He seemed to be getting fit and enjoying doing some work, so it was time to turn him out in the arena, which was 200 by 100 feet, and just let him go for it and be a horse.

Freedom never felt so good....he took off like a rocket.
He was galloping down the side as fast as he could go and would come to a screeching halt in the corner, spin around, kick out, and then take off again. He was bucking, swerving, rearing, and spinning with no balance issues at all. Even the head tilt was not as visible. I was elated—it seemed like Marvin was coming back. At this point, I was tentatively contemplating mounting up in a few weeks.

I had been keeping the vets up to date with Marvin's progress throughout his recovery and sent them the video of this first run.

RESILIENCE ON FOUR HOOVES

Stills from the video. Link to video below.

Dr Ceriotti's response was as follows:

"Hi Mrs. Draper. The video of Marvin's first turnout made me so, so happy. He looks gorgeous, has great energy, and has great body condition as well. I'm really impressed. Thank you for your patience and dedication to him. I'm so glad that he's back in great shape for you both to enjoy your future together."

Watch the video of Marvin's first turnout after the accident: http://www.suzannedraper.com

At this point, there still was no real consensus that Marvin could ever be ridden again, let alone competed, but after watching him run so confidently like this with no ataxia at all I was sure he was going to make a full recovery. With that in mind, I was now contemplating mounting up in a few weeks.

Tentatively Saddling Up and Riding

January 16th, 2023

The morning of the 16th was the day!! It was time to hop on and see how things went. Up to this point, I had been lungeing and working him in the arena, getting him ready for the big day, and so it was time to just do it.

So I popped him on the lunge again and we did some walk-trot-canter both directions, and he seemed to be fine. I took his lunge gear off and mounted, hoping for the best.

I was asked if I was concerned or scared about getting on that first time and really I wasn't. I was not worried at all about his balance but maybe a little anxious about how he would handle my weight on his back again.

We started with walk, some walk circles, and then we trotted and did some trot circles. We halted and just did a whole lot of basics, similar to what we had been doing before the accident, and it was wonderful. He was a little tentative to start off with, but he really settled down, listening to what I was asking, and for that first ride I didn't ask for too much.

He was on the aids better than I imagined he would be, a little apprehensive at first because I had only really ridden him for six months before the accident. I was so thrilled with the ride and how calmly he responded. There were no problems at all. It was terrific. This first ride was only about 10 minutes, but it was enough to convince me I was on the right path and should carry on. I was elated, I never imagined he would go so calmly. It was almost as if he was enjoying finally having something to do.

This was my comment on the video immediately after the ride:

"This is Marvin's first ride since his brain injury, which was the 27th of May last year, 2022, and he is awesome. He has been recovering steadily and I've been lungeing a lot, doing a lot of groundwork, and today was our first ride and he did super. He's just an amazing horse and such a beauty. Love him. He felt really good.

There was no wobbliness or ataxia. He was a little hesitant, because I only just started training him about 6 months before the accident, he's only 5 years old now, but he felt terrific and he's light, he's listening to my legs, he was bending a little off at some points but hey, we're going to work from here."

Watch the video of the first ride:
http://www.suzannedraper.com

I was interested in sending this to Dr Ceriotti to get her opinion because she had initially said, be very careful the first time you get on. I took her advice. So I sent the video to Auburn, and everyone who had worked on him at the hospital was able to see the ride, and this was Dr Ceriotti's comment:

"Mrs. Draper, Thank you very much for sending the video, I agree with you he does really look great while ridden! I'm so happy."

Lungeing before first ride.

First Ride

That gave me a lot of confidence and made me even more determined to start revving things up a little. I continued working him in the same manner, increasing the duration and also the difficulty of what we were doing.

Mostly I worked on the basics, lots of circles, transitions in walk, trot and canter, keeping him relaxed, calm and supple, maintaining a good connection. This was our workout each time I rode and I gradually added complexity for him with leg yields and shoulder in. Everything seemed to be progressing smoothly but as always, any progress is two steps forward and one step back.

Setbacks and Patience

Since bringing him home, there were no really big setbacks. He would keep knocking bits of skin off his eye or up near his ear.
A couple of times he had skin off his hips and also off his hocks. He seemed to be knocking into things because he didn't seem to have the correct spatial awareness of where things were.

His head tilt was still apparent, especially when he was standing in his stall. Nothing seemed to bother him too much. He was getting a little better most days, but of course, some days we'd have a day that wasn't so good where he would be reactive and not want to go forward or didn't want to bend.

Around February 2023, he started having big issues when riding in the arena when he'd hear something in the woods, which were next to the arena. He would react and shy away from the woods, sometimes spinning a few times. It was quite unsettling for both of us and I really wasn't sure what was going on. I kept observing him and trying to work out the issue.

When he was in his stall, I noticed that he had more of a neck and head tilt than he did outside. When riding he was tilting a little but I was able to correct it by bending him.

It definitely wasn't easy for him and I had to ask much more than I normally would but he was getting straighter when ridden. I felt the head tilt was related to him simply building back his strength.

Marvin's head tilt to the right facing the back of the stall.

Something that really caught my attention however, was that the head tilt was more apparent when he heard a noise—he seemed unable to decide where it was coming from, so he would tilt his head and neck more to the right, trying to pinpoint the noise. He would also stand in the stall, facing the back wall rather than looking into the aisle, and his head was tilted at that point too.

I watched him doing this, and then I decided to tie him to a tree like the cowboys do just for patience. This way, he could stand outside with noises and activity going on around him, and I could see how he would react.

Where is the sound coming from.

Being tied was not a problem—he stood really well—but if he heard a sound coming from behind, he would turn his whole body. He didn't seem to know where the sound was coming from. As a result, my husband and I researched hearing in horses and discovered that they tend to pinpoint something from behind using both ears for audio triangulation. At this point, it appeared Marvin was not able to identify audio direction, so we figured he might have a hearing issue.

He was almost due for his 12-month checkup at Auburn Veterinary Hospital, so we decided to ask for him to have a hearing test. The university conducted a BAER test (Brainstem Auditory Evoked Response) on both ears, and sure enough, it appeared he was deaf in his right ear. The results showed almost a flat line on the right ear with the left ear trace appearing normal.

The report on Marvin's BAER Test was: *"As we discussed, Marvin's BAER revealed loss of hearing in his right ear. The test, however, could not quantify the amount of hearing loss*

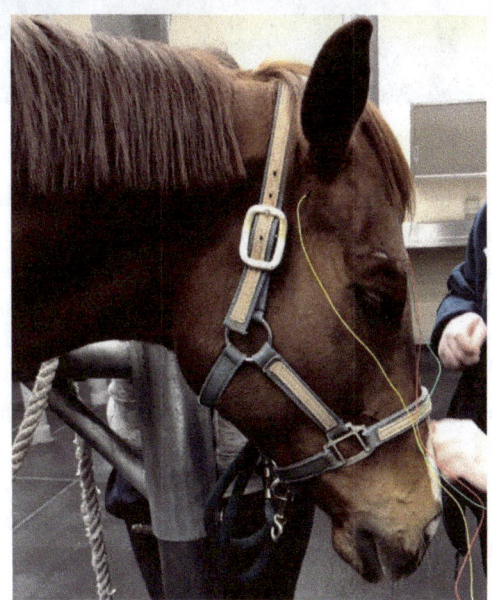

Marvin during BAER Test

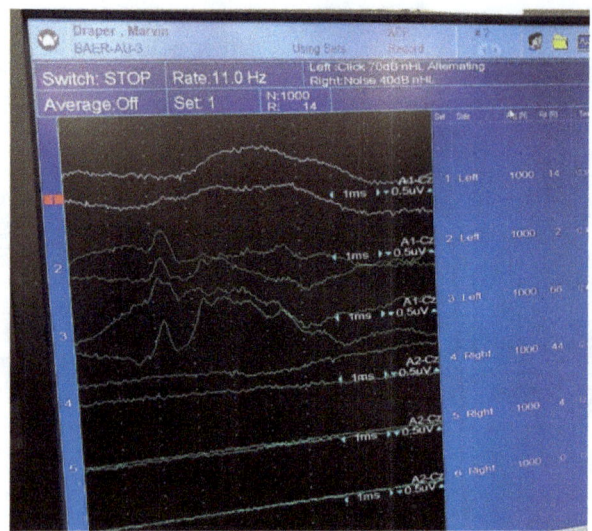

BAER Test Chart

This seemed to partially explain the head tilt and his inability to distinguish where sounds were coming from. At the same time, Marvin had an extremely thorough neurological examination. It was now March 2023, 10 months after the accident.

The report was extensive, a synopsis and the conclusion were as follows:

"Dynamic examination revealed almost complete resolution of the previous abnormalities.

No proprioceptive deficits, proprioceptive ataxia, or vestibular ataxia were observed, even when he was challenged through walking backwards, walking in circles, serpentines, walking up and downhill, and over the curb."

Recommendations included: *"Exercising and riding horses with previous reported brain injury always represent a risk. However, considering the neurological exam results at this visit, Marvin's dynamic neurological abnormalities appear almost completely resolved.*
Thus, progressive reintroduction to riding exercise can be considered. We recommend that Marvin is exercised or ridden only by an adult, experienced riders who are aware of his previous injury."

The BAER Test (Brainstem Auditory Evoked Response) measures the brain's response to sound and helps identify hearing loss. Small electrodes are placed on the horse's head, and sound is played through earphones in each ear. The electrodes detect the brain's electrical responses to the sound, and the results help determine if the horse has any hearing issues. It's a painless and non-invasive test that provides clear insights into how well the auditory pathways are working.

Moving Forward

Following the positive neurological exam, the official go-ahead to start riding, and the newfound knowledge that Marvin did have an unknown degree of hearing loss, I felt I could finally start moving forward knowing where the road was leading. For a couple of months everything seemed to be progressing well during our rides with Marvin having minor spooks or stops to look at something.

Then on May 30th 2023, thinking we were moving rapidly forward, we took another two steps back.

From my Diary Tuesday, May 30th: Hopped on Marvin and he was fine for the first 10 minutes. Then he freaked at something in the woods.

He spun left and then right, back and forth across the arena. When he finally stopped spinning, he was still shaking and tense. I had to wait a minute for him to calm down before I was game to get off. I walked him over to the side and he ran into me and knocked me over. So I lunged him in the arena, then took him outside near the woods until he finally calmed down. I then let him go in the round pen and just let him run. Oh my God, what do I do? Talk with Dr Ceriotti?

I called Dr. Ceriotti the next day and told her about the episode. I was wondering if earplugs might help and wanted to know her opinion or if she had any other suggestions.

We decided it may be worth experimenting with earplugs so any strange noises, especially from behind him, would be muted or completely removed. I ordered the earplugs and two weeks later put them in both ears and saddled up.

The difference was quite noticeable. Marvin was nowhere near as reactive, and riding became much more "normal." I was still being careful and not taking anything for granted, but it felt like we were back—or at least well on the way to a recovery that would allow me to see if Marvin could fully reach his potential.

Three cheers for earplugs.

Chapter 6: Lessons Learned

The journey with Marvin has been one of the most emotionally and physically challenging experiences of my life. From the initial shock of his brain injury to the months of rehabilitation, the setbacks, and the moments of triumph, I have learned an incredible amount—not only about horses but also about myself. Here are some of the key lessons that I have taken from this experience:

1. Patience is Paramount

Perhaps the most important lesson throughout this entire process has been the need for patience. Brain injuries are unpredictable, and recovery is rarely linear. There were times when I would see small improvements, only to experience a step backward the next day. Early on, I realized that Marvin's recovery would be slow, and I would need to adjust my expectations. Patience became a daily practice, whether it was waiting for his neurological symptoms to improve, his eye to heal, or simply giving him the time and space to process new stimuli.

2. The Importance of Observation

Closely observing Marvin every day was critical to understanding his progress.
Noticing his head tilt, his reaction to sounds, his body posture, and his balance allowed me to identify potential issues and work on them before they became bigger problems. Being attentive to the small details—like his reactions to noises or his walking patterns—helped me adapt his rehabilitation program. Every horse is different, and close observation allowed me to tailor Marvin's care to his specific needs.

3. Flexibility in Approach

I came into this journey with little to no idea of what Marvin's recovery would look like.

However, I quickly learned that being flexible and adapting my approach was essential. What worked one week might not work the next. When I saw Marvin struggling with noise or balance issues, I had to modify his training to help him regain confidence.

Taking things day by day allowed me to stay grounded and keep Marvin progressing, even when we faced unexpected challenges.

4. The Value of Professional Support

Throughout Marvin's recovery, I leaned heavily on the expertise of the Veterinary Doctors at Auburn Veterinary University. Their knowledge and guidance were invaluable, from diagnosing his condition to advising on his treatment plan.

The BAER test, the neurological examinations, and the regular checkups at Auburn Veterinary Hospital gave me a clearer picture of Marvin's condition and helped guide my decisions. I also relied heavily on regular chiropractic visits, which gave me insights into how Marvin's body was rebalancing and what areas required more focus. Without this professional support, I wouldn't have had the confidence to continue pushing forward with Marvin's rehabilitation.

5. Listening to Your Horse

While I relied on the advice of experts, I also learned the importance of listening to Marvin.

He would communicate when he was ready for more and when he needed a break. Some days, Marvin was eager to work, while other days, he was more hesitant or reactive.

Paying attention to his mood, energy levels, and body language helped me gauge how much I could ask of him on any given day.
Horses, especially those recovering from trauma, need to be heard. They can't tell you in words how they feel, but their body language and reactions speak volumes.

6. Faith and Determination

One of the most difficult lessons was maintaining faith in Marvin's recovery, even when the odds were against him.

RESILIENCE ON FOUR HOOVES

Many people suggested euthanasia due to the cost and uncertainty surrounding his future, but I believed that Marvin deserved a chance. I was given a constant barrage of "advice" from different people: "Why spend time and money on Marvin when you have no idea of the outcome?" or "It would be easier to put him down and move on, just buy another horse." But I could not bring myself to take any of those paths.

Marvin is such a sweet horse—so relaxed and kind. Even before the accident, we had a very close bond, which only grew stronger during his time in the ICU.

I visited him every other day, despite it being a 3-hour round trip. Even though I could only spend about 20 minutes with him, as I couldn't take up the vet's time, I wanted Marvin to know I was there for him and that I hadn't abandoned him. I was the only person he knew and trusted.

It wasn't blind optimism—it was a belief in his resilience and my ability to help him. Staying determined, even when faced with tough decisions, was crucial to getting Marvin to where he is today.

7. Celebrate the Small Wins

Throughout this journey, I learned to appreciate and celebrate every small victory. Whether it was Marvin standing steadily, reacting calmly to a noise, or trotting without stumbling, these small moments of progress added up over time. It's easy to get lost in the bigger picture, but recovery—especially from something as severe as a brain injury—is about stringing together those small wins.

8. Recovery Isn't Always Physical

While much of the focus was on Marvin's physical recovery—his ability to walk straight, his coordination, and his response to training—there was also an emotional aspect to his rehabilitation. The accident affected him mentally as well. He became more reactive, more cautious, and more sensitive to his surroundings. Helping him regain his confidence and trust took just as much effort as working on his physical recovery.

Just being there twice every day for Marvin was so important. He became very bonded to me, and if unsure about something that was happening, he would immediately look to me for reassurance. I learned that healing is holistic, and emotional recovery is just as important as physical progress.

9. The Power of a Strong Support System

I could not have gone through this experience alone. From the vets at Auburn Veterinary Hospital to my husband, friends, and fellow equestrians, I was fortunate to have a strong support system. The emotional rollercoaster of caring for a horse with such a severe injury is difficult, and having people to lean on made the journey more bearable. Whether it was advice, moral support, or simply someone to talk to, I realized how crucial it is to have people in your corner.

10. There Is Always Hope

The greatest lesson I learned from Marvin is that there is always hope, even in the darkest moments.
When Marvin was first injured, the future looked bleak. The prognosis was uncertain, and I didn't know if he would ever recover enough to be ridden again. But day by day, Marvin showed me that recovery, while slow, was possible.

His determination and will to keep going inspired me to keep moving forward. His story is a testament to perseverance, and it has reinforced my belief that, no matter how dire things may seem, there is always hope.

SUZANNE DRAPER

Chapter 7: The Road Ahead & Conclusion

As Marvin's recovery continues, I am filled with both gratitude and cautious optimism for what lies ahead. Marvin's recovery has been much faster than I imagined particularly when the Vet's had indicated he may never recover. Now, looking forward, I can reflect on both the challenges and triumphs that have defined this experience and what they mean for our future.

The Road Ahead

Marvin's recovery has been slow but steady. After the positive neurological exam and confirmation of his hearing loss, I knew we could start taking more steps forward with his training. Every day with Marvin now feels like a bonus—each ride, each milestone is a victory that I don't take for granted. Even though we've come a long way, I recognize that the road ahead will still have its challenges.

Brain injuries take time to fully heal, however given his progress to this point I am confident he is going to recover fully.

That said, I feel more hopeful than ever. After months of groundwork, physical therapy, and close observation, Marvin has shown me time and again that he is willing to keep moving forward. While we may never reach the competitive heights I once dreamed of, just having Marvin healthy and happy is the most important thing to me now.

Every stride he takes with confidence, every canter without hesitation, is proof that he's still got the spirit and strength that made me fall in love with him in the first place.

In January 2024 I decided to give Marvin a chance to learn to deal with his hearing disability. I turned him out with an older horse so he could just be a horse and become accustomed to the hearing loss and learn to live with it by adapting to the world around him in a natural free environment.

Now, in August, after 8 months and seeing the progress he has made I am going to start putting him back to work. I have been visiting him regularly during his turnout, bringing him in to groom and check him over. One day I couldn't resist and hopped on him bareback. He was so chilled it was like I had been riding him non stop.

Nothing is phasing him, even saddling him was no problem.

He is no longer bothered by unusual or loud noises and seems to have come to terms with his hearing loss taking everything in stride. The plan is to now, after 2 ½ years, to put him back slowly into full work.

Learning to Adapt

One of the biggest lessons I've learned through this journey is the importance of adapting to change.

While it's easy to focus on what we've lost—time, opportunities, and the vision of what our future together would look like—I've learned to appreciate what we've gained. Marvin's recovery has strengthened our bond in ways I never imagined. We've had to adapt to new limitations, and I've learned to adjust my expectations. However, I've also learned to celebrate the progress we make, no matter how small. From this point forward I am going to put Marvin into work, treat him as I would any other horse and explore his capabilities.

Conclusion: A New Perspective

This experience has given me a new perspective on life, horses, and recovery. I now know that success isn't always about winning or reaching a specific destination.

Sometimes, success is about simply showing up, putting in the work, and staying committed to the process, no matter how difficult or uncertain it may be.

Marvin's story is a testament to the strength of the equine spirit, but it's also a reflection of how much we, as horse owners and caretakers, can impact their lives through love, dedication, and belief in their potential. Every small step forward, every bit of progress, is a victory. Marvin may not fully understand the significance of his journey, but I see it in every ride, every interaction, and every moment we share together.

RESILIENCE ON FOUR HOOVES

Looking back, I can say with certainty that this journey has changed me. It has tested my patience, my faith, and my determination, but it has also deepened my love for Marvin.

He has always been the sweetest natured horse which was largely why I was not prepared to give up on him. We are even closer than ever, which I can see each time I go out, as I can simply call his name, he looks up and comes straight to me no matter where he is in the paddock. He is not quite so easy for others to catch, he even missed out on a foot trim because no-one could catch him.

As we move forward, I am filled with unwavering optimism, knowing that Marvin will not only recover but thrive. Together, we will forge a future that is even brighter than I had once imagined, redefining what is possible with each step forward. This journey has shown me that with perseverance, hope, and a bond as strong as ours, even the loftiest of dreams can be reshaped, renewed, and ultimately realized.

SUZANNE DRAPER

Chapter 8: Understanding Brain Injuries

Brain injuries in horses are a critical but often under-discussed aspect of equine health. These injuries can arise from a variety of traumatic incidents, leading to significant changes in behavior, physical capabilities, and overall quality of life. For horse owners, trainers, and caretakers, understanding the nature of these injuries is crucial. This chapter aims to provide an in-depth look at equine brain injuries, including their types, symptoms, diagnosis, and treatment options.

What Is a Brain Injury?

A brain injury in horses occurs when the brain experiences trauma, leading to damage of varying degrees. This trauma can stem from external forces, such as falls, collisions with other horses or objects, or blunt force impacts. The resulting injury may range from mild concussions to severe conditions that require immediate medical attention.

Mechanism of Injury:

When a horse experiences a significant impact to the head, the brain may collide with the skull.

This can cause direct damage at the site of impact and create a contrecoup injury, where the brain is injured on the opposite side due to the violent movement. Understanding these mechanisms helps caretakers prevent injuries through better management practices.

Types of Brain Injuries

1. Concussions:

- Description: A concussion is a mild form of brain injury resulting from a blow to the head. It can disrupt normal brain function, leading to temporary symptoms.
- Symptoms: Common signs include disorientation, lethargy, and mild ataxia (loss of coordination). Most horses recover with proper rest and monitoring.
- Management: Immediate veterinary evaluation is recommended to rule out more severe injuries, and treatment typically involves rest and gradual reintroduction to activity.

2. Contusions:

- Description: A contusion is essentially a bruise on the brain, resulting from the brain being pushed against the skull during impact. Contusions can vary in severity and may result in more pronounced symptoms.
- Symptoms: Affected horses may show significant behavioral changes, prolonged lethargy, or difficulty with coordination.
- Management: Treatment can involve anti-inflammatory medications, strict rest, and regular veterinary monitoring to track recovery.

3. Lacerations:

- Description: This severe form of brain injury involves tearing of brain tissue, often due to penetrating trauma or extreme blunt force. Lacerations can lead to serious neurological deficits.

- Symptoms: Symptoms may include seizures, severe disorientation, and loss of motor function. Horses may also exhibit changes in appetite and social behavior.
- Management: Lacerations typically require urgent medical intervention, possibly including surgery to repair the damage. Long-term rehabilitation may be necessary.

4. Cerebral Edema:

- Description: Swelling of the brain tissue can occur after any type of brain injury, potentially exacerbating existing damage and leading to increased intracranial pressure.
- Symptoms: Symptoms may include severe behavioral changes, seizures, and impaired consciousness.
- Management: Treatment usually includes medications to reduce swelling, such as diuretics, and close monitoring in a veterinary facility.

Common Symptoms of Brain Injuries

Recognizing the signs of a brain injury early can be crucial for effective treatment. Here are some common symptoms to watch for:

- **Changes in Behavior**: Horses may exhibit confusion, agitation, or lethargy. Sudden changes in temperament, such as increased irritability or anxiety, can be warning signs of a brain injury.
- **Coordination Issues**: Difficulty with balance and coordination can manifest as stumbling, weaving, or an inability to execute normal movements. Owners may notice their horse struggling to navigate familiar terrain.

- **Sensitivity to Light and Sound**: Horses with brain injuries may display signs of distress when exposed to bright lights or loud noises. They might shy away from light sources or exhibit increased startle responses.
- **Seizures**: In severe cases, seizures can occur, requiring immediate veterinary intervention. Seizures may present as twitching, loss of consciousness, or uncontrolled movements.
- **Altered Vision**: Horses may exhibit changes in their ability to see or respond to visual stimuli, including an inability to track objects, dilated pupils, or an abnormal response to light.

Diagnosis

Diagnosing a brain injury in horses typically involves a multi-faceted approach:

1. **Neurological Exams**: A veterinarian will conduct a thorough neurological examination, assessing balance, reflexes, and sensory responses. This includes checking for responses to stimuli and evaluating the horse's coordination.

2. Blood Tests: Blood tests may help identify underlying conditions, such as infections or metabolic disorders, that could contribute to neurological symptoms. Elevated levels of certain enzymes or inflammatory markers can provide clues about the horse's condition.

3. Imaging Techniques: Advanced imaging techniques, such as CT scans or MRIs, can provide detailed images of the brain, revealing the extent and type of damage. This imaging is crucial for formulating an effective treatment plan.

4. Observation and History: Gathering a complete history of the horse's behavior and any events leading up to the injury can help in diagnosis. Owners should note the timing and nature of any symptoms observed.

Treatment Options

The treatment of brain injuries in horses varies based on the severity and type of injury. Key approaches include:

1. Rest and Rehabilitation: Rest is essential for recovery. Horses should be kept in a quiet, low-stress environment to minimize stimulation. Gradual reintroduction to activity, based on veterinary guidance, is crucial for effective recovery.

2. Medications:

- Anti-inflammatories: Non-steroidal anti-inflammatory drugs (NSAIDs) may be prescribed to reduce pain and inflammation.

- Seizure Control: In cases where seizures occur, medications such as phenobarbital may be prescribed to manage and prevent further seizures.

- Diuretics: If cerebral edema is present, diuretics can help reduce swelling and alleviate pressure within the skull.

3. **Physical Therapy**: Rehabilitation exercises can help restore movement and coordination. Techniques may include balance training, controlled walking exercises, and even hydrotherapy, depending on the horse's condition.

4. **Nutritional Support**: Maintaining a balanced diet during recovery is important. Some veterinarians may recommend supplements that support brain health, such as omega-3 fatty acids or antioxidants.

5. **Ongoing Monitoring**: Regular veterinary check-ups are essential to track recovery progress and adjust treatment plans as needed. Maintaining open communication with your vet about any changes in behavior or health is vital.

Conclusion

Understanding brain injuries in horses is essential for effective management and care. Early recognition of symptoms, thorough diagnosis, and prompt veterinary intervention can significantly influence recovery outcomes.

RESILIENCE ON FOUR HOOVES

As horse owners and caretakers, being informed and vigilant not only helps in managing injuries but also empowers us to provide the best possible care for our equine companions. Through a combination of medical intervention, rehabilitation, and emotional support, we can help our horses navigate the challenges of recovery and reclaim their joy in life.

SUZANNE DRAPER

Resources

Veterinary and Equine Health Organizations

1. American Association of Equine Practitioners (AAEP)
Website: www.aaep.org
Provides educational resources on equine health, including topics like neurological conditions, injury prevention, and recovery.
2. Auburn University College of Veterinary Medicine
Website: www.vetmed.auburn.edu
Offers equine services, including neurological care and advanced diagnostic techniques for complex injuries.
3. Cornell University College of Veterinary Medicine
Website: www.vet.cornell.edu
Specializes in equine health, with a focus on neurology, surgery, and recovery resources.
4. The Equine Hospital at Rood & Riddle
Website: www.roodandriddle.com
One of the leading equine hospitals in the U.S., known for advanced medical and surgical care for horses.

Books and Educational Materials

1. Equine Injury, Therapy, and Rehabilitation by Mary Bromiley
A comprehensive guide to understanding common equine injuries and the rehabilitation process.
2. Understanding Equine Neurological Disorders by Catherine Willoughby, DVM
A practical resource for horse owners dealing with equine neurological conditions, including brain injuries.

3. The Complete Equine Veterinary Manual by Tony Pavord and Marcy Pavord
Offers practical advice for horse owners on a range of veterinary topics, including rehabilitation for injured horses.

Online Forums and Support Groups

1.Horse Care & Rehabilitation Forum – The Chronicle of the Horse
Website: www.chronofhorse.com/forum
An active community where horse owners can ask questions, share experiences, and seek advice from others on equine care and rehabilitation.
2.Equine Neuro & Rehabilitation Group on Facebook
A support group for horse owners dealing with neurological issues and recovery.

Equine Rehabilitation Centers

1. The Sanctuary Equine Rehabilitation Center
Website: www.sanctuaryequinerehab.com
Specializes in post-injury rehabilitation for horses, with facilities designed to promote recovery and wellness.
2. Equine Rehabilitation Central
Website: www.equinerehabcentral.com
A directory of equine rehabilitation facilities and professionals across the U.S., offering a variety of rehabilitation services, including neurological recovery.

Emergency Equine Services

1. Veterinary Emergency and Critical Care Society (VECCS)
Website: www.veccs.org
Provides a list of veterinary emergency services, with a focus on critical care for horses.
2. On Call: AAEP's Emergency Resource for Horse Owners
Available via AAEP to provide emergency assistance for horse owners needing guidance or veterinary referrals.

These resources are designed to help horse owners better understand and navigate the challenges of brain injuries and rehabilitation, as well as general equine health. Let me know if you'd like to add any additional resources or adjust this list!

SUZANNE DRAPER

About The Author

Suzanne riding Westerley on her property in Maine

Suzanne Draper grew up in Sydney, Australia, in a non-horsey family, yet her passion for horses began at an early age. From the age of 8, she spent every weekend at a farm in **Freemans Reach**, 100 miles from Sydney, where she became actively involved in Pony Club. There, she learned all the essentials of horsemanship, laying the foundation for her future in equestrian sports.

During her years at the farm, Suzanne became an instructor, helping to train and develop numerous horses and riders. Her dedication to teaching and her hands-on experience deepened her knowledge of horsemanship, allowing her to foster strong connections with both horses and students alike.

Suzanne owned several Thoroughbreds when she moved to **Wagga Wagga** in southern New South Wales to attend teachers college. It was during this time that her focus shifted more clearly toward dressage and Three-Day Eventing, as she began honing her skills in these disciplines.

After relocating to the United States with her husband for a career move, she imported two German Warmbloods (Hanoverians), Bastienne and Westerley. She developed Bastienne to successfully compete at the Prix St. George level in dressage.

For Suzanne, the relationship between horse and rider has always been paramount. She places great importance on understanding the emotional and psychological bond that connects them. This deep bond became the driving force in Marvin's recovery after his severe brain injury. Suzanne's unwavering belief in that connection has guided her through the challenges of his rehabilitation, pushing her toward a positive outcome for both her and Marvin.

RESILIENCE ON FOUR HOOVES

SUZANNE DRAPER

www.ingramcontent.com/pod-product-compliance
Lightning Source LLC
Chambersburg PA
CBHW070511090426
42735CB00012B/2741